# GARFIELD'S
## Guide to
# LASAGNA
### COOKING NATURE'S
# PERFECT FOOD

### Rebecca E. Hirsch

Garfield created by JIM DAVIS

Lerner Publications ◆ Minneapolis

Lerner Publications Company
An imprint of Lerner Publishing Group, Inc.
241 First Avenue North
Minneapolis, MN 55401 USA

For reading levels and more information, look up this title at www.lernerbooks.com.

Main body text set in Billy Infant regular.
Typeface provided by Sparky Type.


**Library of Congress Cataloging-in-Publication Data**

Names: Hirsch, Rebecca E., author.
Title: Garfield's guide to lasagna : cooking nature's perfect food / Rebecca E. Hirsch.
Description: Minneapolis : Lerner Publications, [2020] | Includes bibliographical references and
    index. | Audience: Ages 7-11. | Audience: K to Grade 3.
Identifiers: LCCN 2019017252 (print) | LCCN 2019017559 (ebook) | ISBN 9781541583344 (eb pdf) |
    ISBN 9781541572706 (lb : alk. paper) | ISBN 9781541589247 (pb : alk. paper)
Subjects: LCSH: Cooking, Italian. | Cooking (Pasta) | LCGFT: Cookbooks.
Classification: LCC TX809.M17 (ebook) | LCC TX809.M17 H556 2020 (print) | DDC 641.5945—dc23

LC record available at https://lccn.loc.gov/2019017252

Manufactured in the United States of America
1-46537-47582-8/13/2019

# Contents

# HISTORY OF LASAGNA

Lasagna is a dish made with layers of noodles, filling, and sauce. The word itself comes from ancient Greece. The Greeks used the word *laganon* to mean a wide, flat noodle.

Where was lasagna invented? The dish may have come from Italy. But a British cookbook from 1390 has a lasagna recipe. So maybe Britain is the true home of lasagna!

Italy perfected lasagna. At first, tomatoes weren't part of the dish. Tomatoes originally came from South America. Around the sixteenth century,

Spanish explorers brought tomatoes to Europe, and this new food eventually became popular in Italian cooking. When tomatoes met layers of pasta and cheese, lasagna as we know it was born.

Lasagna can be made with all sorts of ingredients. Try inventing your own recipes!

# GETTING STARTED

Ask an adult to be your assistant chef. Some steps are safest with an adult nearby, such as using sharp knives, hot burners, and the oven.

Read the recipe before you begin. Ask your adult helper if you don't understand any of the steps. Be sure to check that you have *all* the ingredients.

Gather your supplies. You'll need the right-sized baking dish, a knife, mixing spoons, measuring cups and spoons, a can opener, a grater, pots and pans, and some bowls.

Be careful when using knives and a grater. They are sharp! Be careful when lifting a hot, heavy pan of lasagna out of the oven too. Always use pot holders or oven mitts. Ask your adult for help if you need it!

Finally, it's a good idea to clean up as you go along. This prevents mountains of dirty dishes when you're done.

IF I HELP CLEAN UP, DO I GET AN EXTRA PIECE?

# OOEY-GOOEY LASAGNA

**This lasagna uses "oven-ready" noodles. Simply place the dry noodles in your dish. No boiling needed!**

### Ingredients

15 ounces (425 g) ricotta cheese

1 egg

½ teaspoon dried basil

½ teaspoon dried oregano

½ tablespoon (7 g) butter

4 cups (946 mL) tomato sauce, divided

12 uncooked "oven-ready" lasagna noodles

4 cups (452 g) shredded mozzarella cheese, divided

¼ cup (25 g) shredded Parmesan cheese

This recipe makes 10 to 12 servings.

1. Preheat the oven to 350°F (177°C). In a bowl, stir together ricotta cheese, egg, basil, and oregano.

2. Lightly butter a 13 × 9-inch pan, and spread ¾ cup (177 mL) of the sauce in the pan.

3. Create the first layer. Place 3 uncooked lasagna noodles over the sauce. The noodles should not overlap or touch the sides of the pan. Spread a third of the ricotta mixture evenly over the noodles. Spread ¾ cup of the sauce over the ricotta mixture, covering noodles completely. Sprinkle with 1 cup (225 g) of the mozzarella cheese.

4. Repeat the layer two more times, creating three layers.

5. Top with the remaining 3 noodles. Spread the remaining sauce on top, covering noodles so they don't dry out. Sprinkle the remaining mozzarella cheese and the Parmesan cheese.

6. Cover with aluminum foil, and bake 40 minutes. Remove the foil, and bake 5 to 10 minutes more, until bubbly along the edges. Remove it from the oven, and let cool 5 minutes. Eat!

NATURE'S MOST PERFECT FOOD

# VERY VEGGIE LASAGNA

**For a healthful addition to lasagna, try vegetables. This version combines veggies and cheese with a white sauce.**

## Ingredients

1 cup (71 g) frozen broccoli, thawed

½ tablespoon (7 g) butter

1½ cups (355 mL) Alfredo sauce, divided

8 uncooked "oven-ready" lasagna noodles

15 ounces (425 g) ricotta cheese, divided

2 cups (226 g) shredded mozzarella cheese, divided

½ cup (15 g) fresh spinach leaves

½ cup (25 g) shredded carrots

¼ cup (29 g) shredded cheddar cheese

VEGGIES, COMING RIGHT UP

This recipe makes 6 to 8 servings.

1. Preheat the oven to 350°F (177°C). Put broccoli in a colander, and squeeze it to remove any water. If broccoli pieces are large, carefully chop into small pieces.

2. Lightly butter 8 x 8-inch baking dish. Spread ¼ cup (59 mL) of the sauce in the pan.

3. Create the first layer. Place 2 uncooked lasagna noodles over the sauce. Make sure the noodles do not overlap or touch the sides of the pan. Spread ⅓ cup (81 g) of the ricotta cheese evenly over the noodles. Sprinkle with ½ cup (56.5 g) of the mozzarella cheese. Sprinkle with broccoli. Spread ¼ cup of the sauce over the broccoli.

4. Make the second layer. Place 2 noodles in the pan, spread ⅓ cup of the ricotta cheese, and sprinkle ½ cup of the mozzarella cheese. Spread spinach leaves over the cheese. Spread ¼ cup of the sauce over the spinach.

5. Make the third layer. Repeat noodles, ricotta cheese, and mozzarella cheese. Sprinkle carrots over the cheese. Spread ¼ cup of the sauce over the carrots.

6. Top with the remaining 2 noodles. Spread the remaining sauce on top, covering noodles so they don't dry out. Sprinkle with the remaining mozzarella cheese and the cheddar cheese.

7. Cover with aluminum foil, and bake 35 minutes. Remove foil, and bake 5 to 10 minutes more, until the top is golden brown. Remove from the oven, and let cool 5 minutes. Eat!

# BERRY BREAKFAST LASAGNA

**Why not try lasagna for breakfast? You can assemble the dish the night before and bake it in the morning. Ask an adult to help you boil and drain the noodles.**

RISE AND SHINE, GARFIELD!

### Ingredients

12 uncooked regular lasagna noodles

12 ounces (340 g) cream cheese

13 ounces (369 g) ricotta cheese

2 eggs

2 tablespoons sugar

⅔ cup (220 g) berry-flavored jam

3½ tablespoons (49 g) butter, divided

2 cups (332 g) berries (blueberries, raspberries, sliced strawberries, or a combination)

This recipe makes 10 to 12 servings.

I'M NOT COMING OUT UNLESS THERE'S LASAGNA

1. Follow the directions on the box to cook the lasagna to a firm, or al dente, stage. Drain in a colander and rinse with cold water.

2. In a bowl, beat together cream cheese, ricotta cheese, eggs, and sugar until smooth.

3. In a small saucepan, heat the jam and butter over low heat until the butter just melts. Stir to combine.

4. Lightly butter a 13 x 9-inch pan, and spread a quarter of the jam mixture in the pan.

5. Make the first layer. Place 3 lasagna noodles over the jam. The noodles can overlap. Spread a quarter of the jam mixture over the noodles. Spread a third of the ricotta cheese mixture evenly over the noodles. Arrange 1 cup (166 g) of the berries over the ricotta cheese.

6. Repeat with another layer of 4 noodles, a quarter of the jam mixture, a third of the ricotta mixture, and the remaining berries.

7. Top with the remaining 4 noodles. Spread the remaining jam mixture over the noodles. Spread the remaining ricotta mixture on top, covering noodles so they don't dry out.

8. Cover with foil and refrigerate overnight.

9. Preheat the oven to 350°F (177°C). Bake lasagna for 40 minutes. Remove the foil, and bake 10 to 20 minutes more, until the top is no longer runny. Remove from the oven. Serve hot or at room temperature.

# PIZZA MEETS LASAGNA

**Combine two of Garfield's favorite foods in one dish.
Pizza and lasagna just naturally go together!**

## Ingredients

15 ounces (425 g) ricotta cheese

1 egg

½ teaspoon dried basil

1 teaspoon dried oregano, divided

½ tablespoon (7 g) butter

4 cups (946 mL) tomato sauce, divided

12 uncooked "oven-ready" lasagna noodles

6 ounces (170 g) pepperoni slices

4 cups (452 g) shredded mozzarella cheese, divided

¼ cup (25 g) grated Parmesan cheese

¼ cup (45 g) chopped green peppers (optional)

¼ cup (40 g) chopped red onions (optional)

This recipe makes 10 to 12 servings.

JUST WHEN I THOUGHT LASAGNA COULDN'T GET ANY BETTER

1. Preheat the oven to 350°F (177°C). In a bowl, stir together ricotta cheese, egg, basil, and ½ teaspoon of the oregano.

2. Lightly butter a 13 x 9-inch pan, and spread ¾ cup (177 mL) of the sauce in the pan.

3. Create the first layer. Place 3 uncooked lasagna noodles over the sauce. The noodles should not overlap or touch the sides of the pan. Spread a third of the ricotta mixture evenly over the noodles. Spread ¾ cup of the sauce over the ricotta mixture, covering noodles completely. Spread a quarter of the pepperoni slices over the top. Sprinkle with 1 cup (113 g) of the mozzarella cheese.

4. Repeat the layering step two more times, creating three layers.

5. Top with the remaining 3 noodles. Spread the remaining sauce, covering noodles completely. Sprinkle with the remaining mozzarella cheese and the Parmesan cheese. Sprinkle with peppers and onions, if using them. Spread the remaining pepperoni over the top. Sprinkle with the remaining ½ teaspoon oregano.

6. Cover with aluminum foil, and bake 40 minutes. Remove the foil and bake 10 minutes more, until bubbly along the edges. Remove from the oven, let cool 5 minutes, and eat!

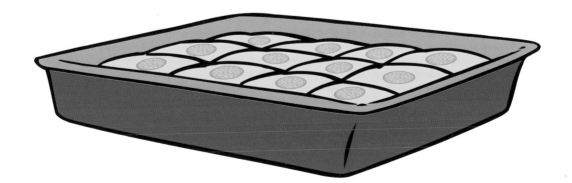

# TERRIFIC TEX-MEX LASAGNA

**Try this yummy, southwestern twist on lasagna.**

## Ingredients

16 ounces (453 g) refried beans

16 ounces (453 g) black beans, drained and rinsed

16 ounces (453 g) corn, drained

1 tablespoon chili powder

1 teaspoon cumin

1 ½ cups (453 g) salsa

15 ounces (425 g) diced tomatoes

½ tablespoon (7 g) butter

4 or 5 10-inch (25-cm) flour tortillas, cut into quarters

3 cups (336 g) shredded Mexican cheese blend, divided

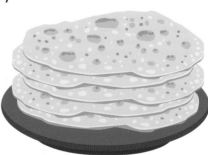

This recipe makes 10 to 12 servings.

1. Preheat the oven to 350°F (177°C). In a bowl, stir together the refried beans, black beans, corn, chili powder, and cumin. In another bowl, stir together the salsa and tomatoes.

2. Lightly butter a 13 x 9-inch pan. Spread ½ cup (293 g) of the salsa mixture evenly over the bottom. Cover the sauce with tortillas. The tortillas can touch or overlap. Spread half of the bean mixture evenly over the tortillas. Then spread ½ cup of the salsa mixture over the beans. Sprinkle with 1 cup (112 g) of the cheese.

3. Add another layer of tortillas. Spread the remaining bean-corn mixture on top. Top with ½ cup of the salsa mixture, and sprinkle with 1 cup cheese.

4. Top with the final layer of tortillas. Spread the remaining salsa mixture on top, and sprinkle with the remaining cheese. Cover with aluminum foil, and bake 45 minutes. Remove from the oven and serve.

HARK! I HEAR THE OVEN TIMER

# ZOODLE LASAGNA

**For an all-veggie alternative to noodles, try zoodles!
Ask an adult to help you cut thin slices of zucchini.
Then sprinkle them with salt to remove the water.**

**Ingredients**

2 zucchini

salt

½ tablespoon (7 g) butter

15 ounces (425 g) ricotta cheese

1 egg

¼ cup (25 g) shredded Parmesan cheese

18 mini frozen meatballs, thawed (optional)

1½ cups (355 mL) tomato sauce, divided

2 cups (226 g) shredded mozzarella cheese, divided

This recipe makes 6 to 8 servings.

1. Slice the zucchini lengthwise into thin strips. Sprinkle generously with salt, and set in a colander to drain. After 30 minutes, spread the zucchini on a clean kitchen towel, roll up the zucchini inside the towel, and squeeze to remove the water and salt.

2. Preheat the oven to 350°F (177°C). Lightly butter a 13 x 9-inch baking dish.

3. Mix ricotta cheese, egg, and Parmesan cheese in a bowl.

4. If using meatballs, cut each one into four pieces.

5. Place a layer of zucchini noodles in the baking dish. Spread half of the sauce evenly over the zucchini. Sprinkle half of the meatballs on top. Spread half of the ricotta mixture over the meatballs. Sprinkle with half of the mozzarella cheese.

6. Repeat the layer one more time. Layer the remaining zucchini, sauce, meatballs, ricotta cheese, and mozzarella cheese.

7. Bake uncovered for 35 to 40 minutes, until the cheese is melted and the lasagna is bubbly along the edges. Let rest for 20 minutes, and then eat!

SO MANY LASAGNAS, SO LITTLE TIME

# CHOCOLATE LASAGNA

**Who says lasagna is only a main dish?
Serve this easy, no-bake lasagna for dessert.**

## Ingredients

2 3.9-ounce packages (110 g) instant chocolate pudding mix

2 cups (473 mL) milk

8 ounces (227 g) whipped topping

16 graham crackers, chocolate or plain

1½ cups (75 g) mini marshmallows

chocolate syrup

This recipe makes 9 to 12 servings.

1. In a bowl, beat the pudding mix and milk together until the mixture is thick and smooth. Gently fold in the whipped topping.

2. Line an 8 x 8-inch pan with 1 layer of graham crackers (about 8 crackers). They can overlap a little. Spread half of the pudding mixture over the graham crackers.

3. Add another layer of graham crackers, and spread the remaining pudding mixture on top.

4. Sprinkle the top with marshmallows. Drizzle a little chocolate syrup over the marshmallows. Refrigerate for at least 1 hour before serving.

A FULL TUMMY IS A HAPPY TUMMY

# LASAGNA ROLL-UPS

**These lasagna roll-ups are easy and cheesy. Have an adult help you boil and drain the noodles.**

## Ingredients

8 uncooked regular lasagna noodles

7 ounces (198 g) ricotta cheese

1 egg

½ teaspoon dried basil

½ teaspoon dried oregano

4 cups (452 g) shredded mozzarella cheese, divided

½ cup (50 g) shredded Parmesan cheese, divided

2 cups (473 mL) tomato sauce, divided

This recipe makes 8 servings.

1. Follow the directions on the box to cook the lasagna to a firm, or al dente, stage. Drain in a colander, and rinse with cold water. Lay noodles side by side on a clean counter or cookie sheet.

2. Preheat the oven to 350°F (177°C). In a bowl, stir together ricotta cheese, egg, basil, oregano, 3 cups (339 g) mozzarella cheese, and ¼ cup (25 g) Parmesan cheese.

3. Using your fingers, spread cheese mixture evenly over noodles until each noodle is covered from end to end. Firmly roll each noodle lengthwise.

4. Spread ¼ cup sauce in an 8 x 8-inch baking pan. Place the lasagna roll-ups seam side down over the sauce. Spread the remaining sauce on top, covering noodles so they don't dry out. Sprinkle with the remaining mozzarella cheese and Parmesan cheese.

5. Bake uncovered for 30 minutes. Remove from the oven. Enjoy!

DID SOMEONE SAY ROLL-UP?

# SENSATIONAL GREEN SALAD

**Add a green salad to complete your meal.**

### Ingredients

1 small head lettuce, torn into bite-sized pieces

*All or some of these:*

8 radishes, thinly sliced

2 carrots, sliced or grated

1 stalk celery, sliced

1 sliced tomato or a handful of
    cherry tomatoes

½ red onion, thinly sliced

½ cucumber, sliced

½ green or red pepper, seeds removed and chopped

Wash and dry the lettuce. Then put the pieces in a big bowl. Sprinkle the other ingredients on top. With salad utensils or your clean hands, mix everything together. Serve with salad dressing on the side.

This recipe makes 4 to 6 servings.

# SHAKE-AND-SERVE ITALIAN DRESSING

**It's fun and easy to mix your own salad dressing.**

**Ingredients**

⅓ cup (80 mL) olive oil

½ cup (120 mL) red wine vinegar

½ teaspoon salt

½ teaspoon pepper

½ teaspoon dried basil

¼ teaspoon dried oregano

FRESH FROM THE FARM!

Put all the ingredients in a jar with a tightly fitting lid. Screw the lid on tight, and shake until the dressing looks cloudy. Enjoy!

# GREAT GARLIC BREAD

**What's lasagna without buttery garlic bread? You can make it with garlic powder or fresh garlic.**

## Ingredients

1 loaf Italian or French bread

5 tablespoons (70 g) butter at room temperature

1½ teaspoons garlic powder or 2 cloves garlic, minced or pressed through a garlic press

¼ teaspoon salt

1. Preheat the oven to 350°F (177°C). Slice the loaf lengthwise.

2. Mix the butter, garlic, and salt in a bowl until creamy. Spread the butter mixture evenly over the cut sides of the bread.

3. Place the bread cut side up on a cookie sheet, and bake 10 to 15 minutes, until golden brown.

4. Remove it from the oven, and cut into 1-inch-thick (2.5 cm) slices. Serve warm.

This recipe makes 6 to 8 servings.

GARLIC BREAD INCOMING!

# YOGURT PARFAIT

**End your meal with a delicious, healthful dessert!**

## Ingredients

2 cups (570 g) Greek yogurt, vanilla or your favorite flavor

2 bananas, sliced

1 cup (166 g) blueberries or sliced strawberries

1. Gather 4 glasses or jelly jars. Spoon ¼ cup (70 g) yogurt into each glass. Arrange half of the banana slices in the glasses. Sprinkle half of the berries over the bananas.

2. Spread the remaining yogurt on top of the berries. Top with the remaining bananas and berries.

This recipe makes 4 servings.

# MEET GARFIELD

**DESCRIPTION:** lazy, lovable cat

**BORN:** in the kitchen of Mamma Leoni's Italian restaurant

**OWNER:** Jon Arbuckle

**FAVORITE FOOD:** lasagna

**LEAST FAVORITE FOOD:** raisins

**FAVORITE DAY OF THE WEEK:** any day but Monday

**FAVORITE PASTIMES:** sleeping, watching TV, and eating Italian food

**DISLIKES:** dogs, Mondays, and empty lasagna pans

29

# Glossary

**bake:** to cook food, covered or uncovered, in an oven

**beat:** to make a mixture smooth by briskly mixing it with a fork, wire whisk, or electric mixer

**chop:** to cut into small pieces with a knife

**colander:** a utensil with small holes for draining food

**fold:** to add a food ingredient to a mixture gently and repeatedly by lifting one part over another

**grater:** a utensil with sharp-edged holes for shredding food into small pieces

**mince:** to cut or chop into very small pieces

**preheat:** to heat the oven beforehand

**tortilla:** a thin, round bread made from cornmeal or wheat flour

# Further Information

America's Test Kitchen. *The Complete Cookbook for Young Chefs*. Naperville, IL: Sourcebooks, 2018.

Cook, Deanna F. *Cooking Class: 57 Fun Recipes Kids Will Love to Make (and Eat!)*. North Adams, MA: Storey, 2015.

Garfield Twitter
https://twitter.com/garfield

Good Housekeeping. *Kids Cook! 100+ Super-Easy, Delicious Recipes*. New York: Hearst Books, 2017.

*National Geographic Kids:* Italy
https://kids.nationalgeographic.com/explore/countries/italy/#italy-coliseum.jpg

PBS Food: Cooking with Kids
http://www.pbs.org/food/theme/cooking-with-kids/

# Index

# Photo Acknowledgments

Design elements: uiliaaa/Shutterstock.com; elvispupy/Getty Images; Big_Ryan/Getty Images; blueringmedia/Getty Images; LplusD/Getty Images; TopVectors/Getty Images; Guzaliia Filimonova/Getty Images; urfinguss/Getty Images; Anna_zabella/Getty Images; Octopus182/ Getty Images; Liubov Khutter-Kukkonin/Getty Images; tashh1601/Getty Images.